WEATHER WONDERS

HURRICANES

HALEY WILLIAMS

PowerKiDS press

Published in 2027 by The Rosen Publishing Group, Inc.
2544 Clinton Street, Buffalo, NY 14224

First Edition

Book Design: Madison Thogmartin

Photo Credits: Cover, p. 1 FotoKina/Shutterstock.com; p. 5 Jeff Schmaltz/NASA; p. 7 hxdbzxy/Shutterstock.com; p. 9 Artsiom P./Shutterstock.com; p. 11 Elizaveta Galitckaia/Shutterstock.com; p. 13 Triff/Shutterstock.com; p. 15 Rawpixel.com/Shutterstock.com; p. 17 ungvar/Shutterstock.com; p. 19 Rix Pix Photography/Shutterstock.com; p. 21 New Africa/Shutterstock.com.

Cataloging-in-Publication Data
Names: Williams, Haley.
Title: Hurricanes / Haley Williams.
Description: Buffalo, NY : Gareth Stevens Publishing, 2027. | Series: Weather wonders | Includes glossary and index.
Identifiers: ISBN 9781538295274 (pbk.) | ISBN 9781538295281 (library bound) | ISBN 9781538295298 (ebook)
Subjects: LCSH: Hurricanes--Juvenile literature.
Classification: LCC QC944.2 W49 2027 | DDC 551.552--dc23

Manufactured in China

CPSIA Compliance Information: Batch #QS27PK. For Further Information contact Rosen Publishing, at 1-800-237-9932.

CONTENTS

What Are Hurricanes?

Hurricanes are powerful **tropical** storms. They are also known as cyclones or typhoons. Hurricanes have strong, **rotating** winds. Heavy rains fall during them. This often causes flooding. These things make hurricanes very **dangerous**.

How Hurricanes Begin

A hurricane begins over a warm ocean. **Humid** air rises from the water. It moves into an area with low **air pressure**. Then it cools. This creates clouds that can turn into a storm. The warm water provides energy for the storm to grow bigger.

As the humid air rises, it rotates. Winds begin circling a center point. This is known as the eye. The winds continue blowing faster. If they reach 74 miles per hour (119 km/h), the storm is a hurricane.

Types of Hurricanes

Hurricanes are put into categories. These are based on how fast the winds blow. The categories go from one to five. Storms above a three are major hurricanes. They cause the most damage. Category Five hurricanes can have winds faster than 157 miles per hour (253 km/h).

Where Hurricanes Happen

Hurricanes usually happen between June 1 and November 30. They form in warm and humid areas of the Atlantic, Indian, and Pacific Oceans. Hurricanes become less powerful in cold water. They also slow down over land. However, they can damage land near coasts.

Damage

Hurricanes can cause a lot of damage. Large amounts of rain can fall. Strong winds also push ocean water onto land. These things can cause flooding. Floods can block roads. People might become trapped. Some may even drown.

Fast winds from hurricanes cause damage, too. The winds can knock down trees and power lines. These may block roads. The power might also go out. Strong winds can knock over buildings. They can also pick up objects. These flying objects can hurt people.

Checking the Weather

Scientists **predict** when hurricanes might happen. **Satellites** track how strong a storm is. They also see where it is moving. Each hurricane is given a name. This makes it easier to share information about it. People near coasts are warned if a hurricane might get close to land.

HURRICANE WARNING
IN EFFECT

Getting Ready

People must prepare for hurricanes. Gathering supplies such as food and water is important. So is checking the weather. Some people may need to **evacuate**. They should go to high ground away from the coast. This is to get away from flooding.

GLOSSARY

air pressure: The weight of air pushing down on an area of Earth.

dangerous: Likely to cause harm or injury.

evacuate: To leave a place of danger to go somewhere safe.

humid: Describing air that is very wet.

predict: To guess that something will happen in the future.

rotating: Spinning around a center point.

satellites: Objects that move around a bigger object, such as a planet.

tropical: Relating to weather that is hot and wet.

FOR MORE INFORMATION

BOOKS

Becker, Trudy. *Hurricane Katrina*. Mendota Heights, MN: North Star Editions, 2024.

Mooney, Carla. *Hurricanes*. Minneapolis, MN: Abdo Publishing, 2025.

WEBSITES

NASA: How Do Hurricanes Form?
spaceplace.nasa.gov/hurricanes/en/
Learn more about how hurricanes form at this website.

Ready Kids: Hurricanes
ready.gov/kids/disaster-facts/hurricanes
Read about what to do before, during, and after a hurricane at this website.

INDEX